MATTIE

8590
8599

Also by G. D. Griffiths

ABANDONED

G. D. Griffiths

MATTIE

The Story of a Hedgehog

ILLUSTRATED BY NORMAN ADAMS

DELACORTE PRESS/NEW YORK

About Hedgehogs

Hedgehogs are small, burrowing mammals found exclusively in Europe, Asia, and Africa. They serve as a natural pest control in gardens, a function similar to that of moles and shrews in America. In appearance, hedgehogs look very much like porcupines with spiky quills, but they are smaller animals.

The text was originally published in Great Britain by World's Work Ltd.

Text copyright © 1967 by G. D. Griffiths
Illustrations copyright © 1977 by Dell Publishing Co., Inc.

Manufactured in the United States of America
First U.S. printing

Library of Congress Cataloging in Publication Data

Griffiths, Gordon Douglas.
    Mattie: the story of a hedgehog.

    SUMMARY: Follows the long, full life of a hedgehog, resident of an English garden, as she grows up, gives birth to several litters, and enjoys her relationship with humans.
        1. Hedgehogs—Juvenile literature. [1. Hedgehogs]
    I. Adams, Norman. II. Title.
    QL795.H4G7 1977   599'.33   76-47240
    ISBN 0-440-05490-7
    ISBN 0-440-05491-5 lib. bdg.

1

IT WAS A warm afternoon in mid-May when old Tom Endacott, scything grass along the edge of a ditch in the grounds of the Old Hall, disturbed two hedgehogs. They tumbled down the steep side of the ditch and ran away into the dead grass and bracken. Tom, who was a kindly man, noticed that the second hedgehog was slow and clumsy, so he decided to leave the rest of the grass along the ditch for another day. He spent the remainder of the afternoon cutting back the tangled mass of creepers that had grown over the toolshed.

The Old Hall, which had been empty for years, had recently been sold, and the new owner had engaged Tom to tidy up the gardens before the family moved in. The Hall itself had already been redecorated, and the windows were opened wide to dispel the smell of new paint and plaster.

When Tom went home for tea, he told his granddaughter Elaine about the hedgehogs.

"Please, Grandpa, let's go and find them. Please, please, please, Grandpa." Elaine was hopping up and down with excitement, and Tom, who could never resist her coaxing, finished his tea and walked with her back to the Old Hall.

The day was slipping into night, but the air was soft and warm and sweet with the scent of hawthorn. It was very pleasant wading through the dead leaves and grasses in the ditch. They disturbed a mouse and some spiders, but there were no hedgehogs to be seen.

Tom showed Elaine a robin's nest built in a piece of old drainpipe. It held a clutch of four red-speckled eggs. They also found a few late primroses hidden along the side of the ditch. Soon it was dark, and Elaine was too tired even to think about hedgehogs. . . .

Later that evening, young Henry Bossom, returning to his cottage, which was about two hundred yards beyond the gates of the Old Hall, saw two hedgehogs creeping into the double hedge between his garden and that of Amelia Dart, his next-door neighbor. Hedgehogs were by no means uncommon in the neighborhood, so he thought no more about them.

The hedgehogs rustled about for a long time. The hedge was full of slugs, snails, and small insects, and the boar was champing until long after moonrise. His pleasure in the abundance of food in his new quarters was only slightly marred by his bewilderment at the behavior of his mate. He thought she must still be frightened by their narrow escape from the scythe; she showed little interest in the juicy morsels that could be found in the undergrowth, and sat panting by the edge of a rotten tree stump.

Later, she climbed painfully into his hollow stump, and he heard her stamping dead leaves into a bed. She came out once or twice during the night to collect dried grass and leaves. He did not know that she was heavy with young and her time was near, but he felt a strange compulsion to stay near her and protect her if need arose.

Soon after dawn, the boar flung himself down to sleep by the cleft leading into the hollow stump. He slept flat on his stomach, as a hedgehog sleeps in summer, knowing that he was well hidden by grass and leaves. The hedge was dry and thick, and he slept peacefully.

Inside the tree stump, the sow slept fitfully on her bed of leaves. Now and then, she rose to stamp the leaves flatter in the middle of the nest, turning round and round like a dog, making a deep, saucerlike depression. She was unhappy and fretful and did not understand the strange forces that drove her. She was only twelve months old, and this would be her first litter.

Next day, when the sun was high overhead, her young were born. There were three of them: two males and a female. The female was born last while the sow was still licking her two sons. She washed all three of them thoroughly with her long, pink tongue and tidied up the nest. The little ones snuggled down in the long, woolly hair along her flank. They were about the size of pennies and had blunt, undeveloped snouts. They had no prickles and they were a naked, grayish-white color. Their eyes were closed under wrinkled brows.

The old boar awakened toward sunset and climbed into the nest. The three young ones were sucking and pushing at their mother with their tiny paws as she lay on her side, relaxed and happy. When she saw the boar, she snarled softly, and when he moved nearer her young, she spat and snapped at him.

That night, he hunted for his food close to the old tree stump. From time to time, he climbed up to the nest and was met with a snarl and a grimace. The young hedgehogs slept, sheltered by their mother's body.

At dawn, the boar went to sleep across the cleft leading into the tree stump. The sow did not stir out of the nest, but from time to time she washed her young, paying particular attention to their eyes and ears, which are susceptible to attacks from maggots. The faint beginnings of bristles were showing on their backs, and when she turned them over to wash their undersides, they opened their mouths in little soundless cries. All day long she nursed and fed them, and when evening came, the boar saw that she slept with her paws across their bodies.

Early the next morning, while her young were still fast asleep, she crept from the nest to search for food, but she was too anxious to stray far. After she had eaten a few wood lice and a couple of luscious slugs, she felt that her hunger was assuaged. While she hunted, for an hour or so at dawn and dusk each day, the boar slept across the sill of the nest.

By the end of the fourth day, the little hedgehogs had opened their eyes and were able to make faint, mewing cries. Their bristles were clearly noticeable; they were rather like the quills left on a badly plucked chicken and of the same grayish-white color. By the end of a week, they had their full complement of soft, gray-white bristles and their bodies had dark-

ened a little. Their snouts were still not fully developed, but they could see and they could crawl around in the nest. Their mother still washed and suckled them.

On the young hedgehogs' tenth day of life, a cat appeared in the hedge. It was the old tomcat that belonged to Amelia Dart, and it crawled along a branch above the hedgehogs' nest. The sow became very agitated, and eventually her snuffling and spitting awoke the boar. Both the adult hedgehogs threatened the cat repeatedly, but it remained crouched on the bough over their heads and there was little they could do. As soon as dusk fell, the sow prepared a new nest at the top end of an overgrown garden some fifty yards further down the line. She carried her young to it one by one, holding them carefully in her mouth, grasped by the tough skin at the base of their necks. She made sure that her sharp teeth did not penetrate their hide.

The boar went out as usual for his evening's hunting, but the sow was still too worried to leave her babies and seek her own food.

The young hedgehogs spent their waking hours exploring their new home. Their bristles were beginning to darken from the roots upward; they were now half gray and half white. Woolly hair was growing on their stomachs, and their snouts and tails were developing rapidly. Their faces and claws had darkened to a grayish-brown.

Quill was larger than the other two, and Mattie had on her side a patch of bristles that had been damaged when her mother was carrying her to the new nest. These bristles remained short and white and looked like a scar on her flank. Although they darkened and grew longer in later life, it was always easy to recognize Mattie by this patch of white-tipped bristles. The third youngster was a nondescript little urchin called Spiky.

As her young grew, the mother was less determined in her efforts to keep the boar from the nest, and when she was hunting one evening he climbed in. The youngsters awakened immediately, and Quill ran toward him, his nostrils working, to find out what this strange creature was. Quill recognized the hedgehog scent, which was much ranker than that of his mother, but he was amazed by the size of this strange animal, with his big buff face with black bands running down each side of the snout.

The boar sniffed at Quill and at each of the youngsters in turn, then shuffled out of the nest. The babies were excited but quite unafraid.

When the mother returned, she realized that her mate had been in the nest, and she washed her babies with great care to see that they were unharmed. After that, the boar often climbed into the nest, and she cared about it less and less.

At the end of the third week, she started to bring her young little delicacies when she returned from hunting. At first, they did not know what to do with the slugs and snails she laid before them. They tried to play with them, but she soon taught them that such things were good to eat.

The youngsters' bristles were now gray, darkening to brown at the base, and white-tipped. The great carnosus muscle in their backs, which would later control the erection of their bristles, had thickened and set, but the tendons were still too weak to allow the little hedgehogs to do more than curl themselves into a prickly semicircle. Their faces were covered with coarse, prickly hair, and their snouts and feet were black. Their short front legs were covered with thick, furry black hair, but their back legs, which were longer and ended in little claws, were only sparsely covered. They kept their tails tucked under them. From head to tail, they were now about two and a half inches in length.

During their fourth week of life, they lived on a mixed diet of slugs, snails, centipedes, wood lice, and other small creatures their mother brought to them. She still suckled them at intervals and would continue to do so until the end of their fifth or sixth week, but her milk was already beginning to dry up.

The boar showed less and less interest in his family and spent more and more time away from the nest. Often he did not sleep there for two or three days at a time. He was a very old hedgehog of some five or six summers, and he quickly forgot about his family in the excitement of hunting in the short summer nights. He needed a lot of food to maintain his bulk; he weighed over two pounds. He was old enough and crafty enough to lie in wait for field mice outside their holes and to steal an occasional bird's egg. He had weathered so many vicissitudes and seen so much of man that he was afraid of very little. Each year he fathered a family, and each year he regarded them with interest and surprise for a few weeks and then forgot about them.

His former mate had died of pneumonia during their winter hibernation, and his present mate was much younger than he. They differed widely from each other: she had dark brown, shiny bristles; a small, black head; and fur-covered legs; while he had a grizzled, fawn-and-black-striped head with prominent ears. His legs were worn bald and he had splay feet with five-toed claws. His bristles were faded and dusty.

The boar had found a garden in which milk was left out each night. He did not know, when he first raided the cat's saucer, that the owner of the garden saw him approaching in the half-light and mistook him for a rat. The man had run for his .22 rifle, which hung, ready-loaded, on the wall, but the hedgehog had felt the vibration of his footsteps and had slunk into cover. For several evenings, the man had looked for the "rat" in the moonlight, but he did not see it.

Then one evening his wife, looking out of the kitchen window, saw the hedgehog at the cat's saucer. He was clearly outlined against the

11

white dish and was easily recognizable. These people had always wanted a hedgehog, for they knew it would clear the garden of pests, so they put out bread and milk, which the hedgehog came for each evening.

The boar ranged over several gardens during the night, but his mate always hunted near the nest. As the young hedgehogs grew stronger, their mother found them less and less easy to control. On one occasion, Mattie was missing when she returned to the nest. She nuzzled the other two youngsters and tried to settle down with them but could not because of her sense of loss. At midday, she could stand it no longer and she climbed from the nest, her nose to the ground, following the scent of Mattie. For a long time she ran fruitlessly up and down the lane, keeping in the shadow of the hedge. Once she saw a man and froze in her tracks, but her anxiety for Mattie was so great that she did not curl up: she waited with her brows wrinkled over her eyes and her spines slightly tensed, her legs bent and her snout tucked down, until the man had passed by. He did not notice her, and she ran on, prying into every patch of nettles and long grass. Eventually she found herself in the bread and milk garden, and there she found Mattie. The little hedgehog had crept out of

the nest during the night and had played by herself until morning. Dew and the morning mist had chilled her, and she felt cold and hungry, but she had wandered so far from home that she could not find her way back. She had run further and further, with her nose to the ground, trying to pick up her own scent, but she had become hopelessly confused. At last she had settled down, exhausted, to sleep in the sunshine. (Although hedgehogs are now nocturnal animals, many thousands of years ago, when there were few men and no vehicles, they hunted freely by day and by night. Even now, a young hedgehog is grateful for the warmth of the sun and loves to bask in it.)

Just before her mother arrived, somebody had come to pick strawberries, and Mattie, awakened suddenly by the footsteps, had fled shrieking down the path. The woman picking the strawberries had thought that the thin, high shrieks had come from a wounded bird, but Mattie's mother knew her cries. Grunting and scolding, she collected her erring baby and shepherded it back to the nest.

She removed a couple of ticks from among Mattie's prickles and gave the little hedgehog quite a vicious shake with her teeth before they settled down to sleep.

~2~

MATTIE was by far the most adventurous of the young hedgehogs. In their fifth week, their mother took them with her to hunt by the light of the moon, and it was always Mattie who broke away from the dutiful, nose-to-tail file and scampered off alone. It was Mattie who found new foods to sample, scratching in the moss and lichen along the garden paths and finding tiny insects. She nosed behind stones and brought out fat yellow slugs, centipedes, and earthworms. Once she caught a moth and ate it, but the dust on its wings made her sneeze.

Hedgehogs are insectivores, but they will eat any meaty creature they can catch. They also eat a very small amount of vegetable matter—crunchy things like the leaves and stems of arum lilies and sometimes lettuce leaves. The small amount of damage they do in a garden is more than outweighed by the pests they destroy. After all, it is better to have a lettuce or two slightly torn than to lose a whole row of seedlings to slugs or snails or to have a crop of broad beans ruined by blackfly.

The little hedgehogs hunted with their mother over five or six gardens, following her with their noses to the ground, so that they walked in her scent. They went the same way each night and learned to know the ground they covered by its pattern of smells. Their mother taught them to walk with their snouts lowered and their bristles slightly raised. She taught them to "freeze" at any sudden noise, but if danger threatened from afar they learned to run and hide themselves under leaves or to stand in the shadow of a rock or a clod of earth. At first, a sudden, bright light would panic them, but their mother taught them to stand still until it had gone and then to run into the shadows. They were still too young to curl themselves into a ball, and they felt very defenseless.

Quill, who usually followed close behind his mother, was always obedient, but the other male, Spiky, who was second in the file, was very nervous and often forgot to "freeze." Mattie, who came last in the line, was just plain naughty.

One night, when the young hedgehogs were

six weeks old, Mattie caught the scent of the old boar upwind of them and broke away from her place in the file to see what he was doing. Ignoring her mother's grunts, she ran off, following the boar's scent. The exasperated sow led the two young boars in pursuit.

The boar, closely followed by the excited Mattie, trotted down the path that led to his supper of bread and milk. He had hardly sunk his forefeet in the saucer before Mattie and the rest of the family arrived. The boar climbed into the saucer, which is the way of hedgehogs when they want to protect their food, and started to eat noisily.

The sow and her young ran around the edge of the saucer, lapping up the spilled milk and occasionally snatching a mouthful of bread or milk from under the boar's hindquarters. He was furious, and his spitting and snarling brought the woman of the house to her kitchen window. All she could see was a mass of dark bodies against the white saucer, so she brought a flashlight and trained it on them through the window. In the beam of the light, four startled pairs of eyes shone green; the boar continued to eat with his back turned. He felt only contempt for humans and all their ways.

When the light went out, the sow, Quill, and

Mattie ran back the way they had come, following their own scents into the shadows, but Spiky panicked and ran around the concrete terrace of the house to the front garden, which adjoined the main road. The noise and the lights of the passing vehicles terrified him still further, and he flung himself, shivering, into a patch of nettles, which stank of cats.

The sow, followed by the other young hedgehogs, tried to trace him, but her fear of the traffic and the stench of cats, which overlaid Spiky's scent, prevented her from finding him. She was forced to return to the nest at dawn without him.

That afternoon, the woman and the man from the bread and milk house found the little hedgehog cowering on their garden path. He cried pitifully when they picked him up. They realized that he was lost, so they filled a large flowerpot with hay and laid it on its side in the back garden near the lane where they knew the hedgehogs lived. They left a saucer of milk beside the flowerpot, but Spiky was far too frightened to eat. He burrowed into the hay and stayed there all that day and night. The next evening, the woman caught the old boar when he came for his supper and put him in the flowerpot beside the baby, thinking that he might comfort Spiky and lead him home, but the boar, in high dudgeon at this interference with his plans, merely lapped up the milk and trotted off.

The little hedgehog grew weaker and was obviously pining for his mother. He refused to take any food; the woman tried to squeeze drops of milk between his teeth, but he sadly turned his head away.

The sow was still trying to find him. She even looked for him in the patch of nettles where he had originally taken refuge, but there was no scent trail to lead her to the flowerpot because Spiky had been carried there. As the days went by, she gradually forgot poor Spiky and concentrated on her other babies.

In six days, Spiky had not stirred from his bed of hay. Each day he had refused to eat, although the woman offered him chopped raw meat, bread and milk, and even cream. His nose, which should have been cool and moist, began to grow dry and hot, and his eyes were hidden under close-packed wrinkles. It was obvious that he was dying, but there was nothing that could be done. He was terrified of life without his mother, and on the seventh day he rolled over on his side and died. They buried him under an apple tree at the end of the garden.

Mattie and Quill were now learning to hunt

without their mother. Each night, they followed the familiar trails, returning to the nest at daybreak. They often reached the saucer of bread and milk before the old boar and stole most of it. The woman of the house realized that she now had a whole family of hedgehogs to feed, so she changed the saucer for a soup plate. Each morning, the plate was marked by the muddy prints of three or four sets of feet, but two sets were always much smaller than the others.

The boar was old and his teeth had lost their sharpness. His sight and hearing were failing, but his sense of smell was still as keen as ever. He was grateful for the bread and milk because the young hedgehogs had eaten most of the slugs, snails, and other food in the gardens. Had he been younger, he would have hunted further afield, but he was set in his ways and a little tired.

One night, after a party at the house, some corned beef sandwiches covered with milk were left in the hedgehogs' plate. The old boar arrived early and found the sandwiches so tasty that he ate them all and licked the plate dry. He had eaten nearly half a small loaf, as well as the milk and the corned beef, so he felt very full indeed. It was all he could do to drag himself into the shelter of the rhubarb patch. He lay on his back, with his legs in the air, his stomach distended like an overfed kitten's. The milkman found him there at seven the next morning and playfully prodded him. The old boar glared malevolently at him from his beady black eyes and scurried off into the hedge.

Mattie had had an adventure, too. She had left the nest in the heat of the afternoon and had set off to explore the hedgerow. It had been raining, and the heat of the sun was bringing all manner of delicious smells out of the damp earth. Since she was not really hungry, she tasted a lot of things that would not normally have interested her. She nibbled some fungus from the roots of a tree, she gnawed at an oak apple, and she bit off the shoot of a young nettle, which she spat out because she did not like its bitter taste. She did not move quietly; hedgehogs do not make any attempt to hide the sound of their movements.

A man called Jack Belton was on his way home from work and heard her rustling in the hedgerow. He soon found her and scooped her up in his handkerchief, thinking she would be useful to have in his garden. He carried her to his house, which was next door to the bread and milk house, and put her in a disused hen coop with a saucer of milk.

When she found herself fastened in the hen

coop, Mattie felt very frightened. Her back muscles contracted, and she curled up into a prickly ball that looked rather like the husk of a sweet chestnut. Jack Belton laughed and called his young son to see the "fuzz-peg," the name given to hedgehogs in Devon.

It was the first time that Mattie had completely curled up, and she was very surprised and proud. She could not stay curled up for long; her muscles were still too weak, and she had not yet learned the trick of breathing sideways through the woolly hair of her stomach. She felt very clever and grown-up, even though she had to uncurl after a minute or two.

That same evening, Jack Belton was bragging in the "Clifford Arms," saying that he had caught a young "fuzz-peg" for his garden and shut it up in the hen coop. But when he got home the milk had gone—and so had Mattie! She had wriggled through the bars of Belton's hen coop and run back to the nest.

~3~

AT THE END of the lane where the hedgehogs lived the land sloped down to the peaty waters of a stream. Fifty years or more ago, clay had been mined from a shelf of land known as The Waste, which stretched along the banks of the stream to the foothills of Dartmoor. Over the years, the workings filled with water and formed a long, narrow lake. This lake was very deep, and it was full of huge eels. On sunny afternoons tench could be seen basking on the surface of the water, and pike lay in the shadows of the over-hanging blackberry bushes. Foxes and badgers lived in the overgrown clay dumps at the edge of the stream, and a family of otters had made its home in a hollow tree at the water's edge.

The winter floods had carried down seed-capsules of balsam from the moor, and the banks of the stream were now screened by a thick growth of these plants. In the heat of the afternoon the cloying scent of their flowers attracted swarms of bees, and at nightfall the place was alive with moths.

Part of The Waste had been fenced off as a meadow, and the little hedgehogs liked to wander over it, searching under dried cowpats for the fat, white maggots that lived there. They liked the warm, sweet scent of the cows and sometimes, in the early hours of the morning, they would lick up a few drops of milk that had oozed from the overfull udder of one of the sleeping animals.

The little hedgehogs were terrified of Playboy, the big shire horse that grazed in this meadow. Sometimes, irritated by the prickly little animals, he would lash out at them with his great hooves as they ran between his feet.

On dewy evenings, they found young frogs in the grass beside the lake, and there were usually pieces of bread and small fish left behind by the anglers who came there during the day.

The old boar was very fond of frogs and fish, but he did not go to The Waste very often; even in his fearless old age, the scent of the fox and the badger alarmed him. He had found too many of his kind split open, with their skins emptied of flesh. The fox, the badger, and the Alsatian dog are the only animals against which the hedgehog's armor of prickles is useless; all three will bite through the curled-up urchin and gorge themselves on the succulent flesh of its body.

As the summer progressed, the old boar grew tired of his diet of bread and milk. He found fewer and fewer slugs and snails in the gardens where he hunted, and his stomach cried out for meat. His mouth watered at the memory of a young rabbit he had found in a snare on The Waste a year or so before.

One evening in August, when the moon was full, he set off for The Waste, followed by the sow and her two young. Quill and Mattie were excited by the unfamiliar scents as they gamboled along, teasing the older hedgehogs unmercifully. They ran through the long grass at the edge of the lake, pouncing on grasshoppers and frogs. . . .

It was Mattie who, rooting under a large stone, disturbed a snake with a black **V** on its head: an adder that had spent the day catching gnats and swimming in the cool waters of the lake. At dusk, it had curled up in the shelter of the stone, which the sun had warmed during the day.

The sleeping adder was annoyed at being disturbed by Mattie, who had never before seen anything like it and sprang back in terror as it uncurled. The old boar pounced on the snake and bit into its side, curling himself up in the same motion. As the adder struck at him, the sow darted in and bit its tail. It struck at the hedgehogs again and again, but its venom wasted itself harmlessly on their bristles. Soon the reptile was exhausted, its poison sacs empty and its throat terribly torn by the old boar's bristles. It tried to slither away, but both adult hedgehogs uncurled and attacked it savagely. They tore the flesh from its still living carcass while Mattie bit fiercely at its tail. The boar chased Quill away when he tried to join in the feast.

The young boar slunk off, feeling very lonely, and hunted along the side of the lake until he came to a slippery patch of clay. The weight of his bristles caused him to overbalance on the steep slope and he fell into the water; but, like all hedgehogs, he was a good swimmer and he soon found a pebbly part of the bank and scrambled out of the lake. He shook himself and licked his chest and stomach with his long, pink tongue. He had lost most of his fleas and lice in the water, and the few that had taken refuge on his head and ears were quickly dislodged by a scratch or two from one of his hind feet. His skin tingled, and he started to lick it again. As he did so, the saliva gathered in his mouth, his head bobbed up and down, and his tongue worked

faster and faster. In an ecstasy of pleasure, he turned his head sharply, throwing big blobs of saliva onto his back. He was performing the age-old rite of self-anointing, a mystery no human understands.

After a while, Quill trotted back and found the other hedgehogs. By then, the adder's bones were picked clean.

At dawn, an angler fishing for tench in the lake found the disjointed vertebrae of the snake. Its head was still intact, though severed from its body, and the man thought that rats must have eaten the flesh from its bones. He returned to his fishing and saw at the edge of the lake a little pike, no more than an inch long, trying to swallow a tiny, silvery roach almost as big as itself. He sat watching his red-tipped float and marveled at the pitiless cruelty of nature.

Mattie and Quill were now almost full-grown. Their mother was running with the old boar again, although the mating season was over. She no longer slept in the nest.

The young hedgehogs continued to go for their supper of bread and milk each evening. They came down the garden path from their nest in the hedge, running and skipping in the shadows, tumbling down the steps and jostling each other at the plate, wading knee-deep in the bread and milk. They ate noisily, their teeth snapping together loudly. They hiccuped, and they sneezed milk from their nostrils from time to time. When they were tired of eating, they chased each other round and round the plate and ran along the concrete terrace of the house looking for insects. When they walked, their longer back legs made them wobble, so that they looked from behind like little brown bears.

They were not afraid of the man and woman who lived in the house and freely allowed them to stroke their noses and foreheads. Mattie was much smaller than Quill, but she was far more intelligent than her brother, and she quickly learned to take a piece of milk-soaked bread from the woman's fingers. She knew the familiar sounds of the house, and she would eat her bread and milk quite happily while the lights blazed and the sound of the radio came through the open window. Both she and Quill seemed to know when there were strangers in the house; they never came near if the woman and her husband had visitors.

They had found the hay-filled flowerpot in which their brother had lived at the end of his short life, and they often spent a night in it, not

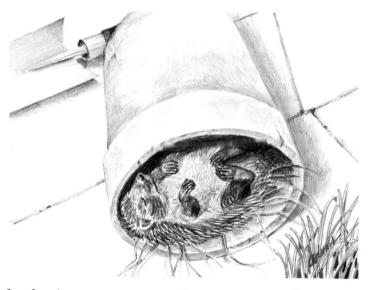

bothering to return to the nest. One afternoon, the man of the house was digging in the garden, and he rolled the flowerpot out of his way with his foot. It rolled for a few feet and came to rest against a stone. He walked over to it to move it again, and inside it, he discovered, was Mattie, stretched out on the hay, her white patch clearly visible. She was breathing calmly and quietly, in no way upset by the rough treatment the pot had undergone. The man gently put the flower-pot back in its old place and packed pieces of slate under it to raise it above the damp of the ground. From then on, it was known as Mattie's pot.

An old man named Bert Smale lived at the

end of the lane, and he was very ignorant of the ways of hedgehogs; he insisted that they dug up and ate potatoes, besides doing other damage in his garden. The year before, he had caught the old boar and thrown him into the dustbin, thinking he had killed him; but the bin was nearly full and the old hedgehog had soon recovered consciousness, clambered up on the rubbish, and pushed off the loose-fitting lid. As he scrambled over the edge of the dustbin, he curled himself up into a ball, and his bristles broke the shock of his fall to the ground. When Smale discovered that the "dead" hedgehog had escaped, his rage knew no bounds.

One evening toward the end of August, the sow was eating a snail in old Bert's potato patch. He saw her in the half-light and rushed at her, brandishing a spade he had snatched from the toolshed as he ran by it. The hedgehog cowered meekly on the ground, waiting for the danger to pass, but Smale sliced her head from her body with a single blow of the spade. He left the pathetic little body in the potato patch as a warning to "the other little varmints, dang 'em."

"I saw 'un. I saw the little varmint with me own eyes. A-digging of me 'taters, he wuz," he told his wife, "but I've finished him off for sure this time."

Old Bert was a keen gardener, and he liked nothing better than to boast in the "Clifford Arms" about all the cups he had won at the local Show; but that year he did not win anything. Long before September twenty-first, the date on which the Show was held, all his best produce had been ruined by slugs and snails.

4

AT THE beginning of September, the hedge-hogs were already preparing to hibernate, and rolls of fat were forming under their thick, woolly coats to protect them from the cold of winter. Their blood was thickening, and the white corpuscles in it were increasing in number. Their glands were secreting antitoxins, and the skin around their mouths and eyes was growing less attractive to maggots and flesh worms. They were eating so much food that they were becoming sluggish and less inclined to play.

Mattie and Quill carried more leaves and hay into their flowerpot. They also took two clothes-pins, an onion, and a button into it, for hedge-hogs, like humans, must have their toys. They stowed their treasures safely away behind the hay and leaves.

Neither of the young hedgehogs had hibernated before, nor had they been taught how to prepare their winter quarters, but they knew instinctively what they had to do. Soon the flowerpot was snug with a thick carpet of leaves under a curtain of hay.

Hedgehogs were originally natives of central and southern Europe, where the long, hot summers and the dry winters are ideal for them. They spread to England thousands of years ago, coming across the land bridge that then joined England and France, and there are now about fifty million of them in Great Britain. They are less common in the north, there are very few of them in the Highlands of Scotland, and they are only just beginning to reach the Western Isles through hibernating families being carried there accidentally in bales of hay. In England's climate, hedgehogs suffer from rheumatism, and they will often die of pneumonia in a cold, wet winter; but they are very adaptable animals and they usually stay healthy if their winter quarters are warm and dry.

The woman from the bread and milk house was very pleased that Mattie and Quill were preparing to hibernate in her garden. She padded the top and sides of the flowerpot with newspaper and covered it with an old sack, and her husband put an old zinc bathtub over all in

such a way that the hedgehogs' winter quarters were protected from rain and wind. He left just enough room for them to crawl in and out under the edge of the bathtub. By the beginning of October, the young urchins had wrapped themselves up in sycamore leaves and had curled up together, ready to sleep the winter away.

The old boar came for bread and milk for a few more evenings; then he, too, looked around for a suitable place to hibernate. He chose an old seed box full of drifted leaves in a derelict greenhouse at the edge of The Waste.

The autumn was fine and dry: the days were bright and sunny, and the nights were crisp with frost. The haws shone scarlet in the hedges and the old men shook their heads as old men do, muttering that it was going to be a hard winter. The brambles on The Waste were laden with purple blackberries, and the hazels were weighed down by their clusters of golden brown nuts. On the hillsides, the plows turned over the rich, red earth, which was quickly dyed to crimson by the autumn dews. The fields spread in a bright patchwork over the landscape until they faded into the purple foothills of Dartmoor. On the moor itself, fires to burn leaves were lit and the sweet smell of their smoke drifted down the valley on the breeze.

On the edge of The Waste, the local boys started to build their fire in readiness for Guy Fawkes Day. They went around to all the houses in the lane collecting old horsehair mattresses, broken-down chairs, old newspapers, and other suitable materials. The boys piled it all up high, with a guy, made from a straw-packed old suit crowned by a turnip head, on top. The guy had catherine wheels pinned to its cheeks, and it was "smoking" a Roman candle. There was an old trilby hat perched on its turnip head.

When the fire was lit, it blazed fiercely for a time; but the material of which it was made was so dry that the flames soon began to die down, so the boys set off to find more things to throw onto it. They fastened ropes around an old tree stump and dragged it to the fire, but the stump was too damp to burn at once, and they decided to go to the derelict greenhouse for something dry to start it off. The boys tore down the shelves of the greenhouse and dragged out the pile of old seed boxes. They were just going to throw this new material onto the fire when one of them saw the old boar curled up in the dry leaves that lined one of the seed boxes.

"There's an old fuzzy-peg," he yelled. The noise woke the old boar, and he uncurled enough for the boy to grab him by his hind legs. He flexed his back and sank his teeth deep into his tormentor's wrist.

The boy dropped him with a scream of pain, and as the hedgehog fell to the ground, he curled up again, cushioning his fall with his bristles.

The boy, who until then had looked on it as a bit of fun, grew angry and spiteful. Holding his injured wrist with his other hand, he kicked out wildly at the old boar, sending him into the heart of the bonfire. The unfortunate animal uttered a loud, wailing cry of pain as the flames seared into his bristles.

The cruel boy did not get off scot-free; the teeth of an old hedgehog are often poisonous, and his wrist became infected. He was in the hospital for nearly three weeks.

⌒5⌒

THE WEATHER was fine and mild until after Christmas; most nights there was a touch of frost, but the wind blew steadily from the west and the temperature did not fall very low.

At the beginning of January, daffodils and violets were in leaf, and snowdrops filled every hollow. The mild air woke the hedgehogs, and for a few evenings the woman from the bread and milk house found them patiently waiting with their snouts pointed toward the place where their plate used to be put.

When she had given them their food, they would run off to hunt in the gardens, but they always returned to their flowerpot before dawn.

Then suddenly, when the earth seemed to be trembling on the brink of spring, winter struck. The thermometer fell twenty degrees overnight, and the land woke up to a bitter east wind and a black frost. The temperature rose a little during the day and an inch or so of snow fell, but by nightfall ten degrees of frost had turned the snow to solid ice. On The Waste, the lake was frozen hard, and the fish sought refuge in the mud at the bottom. The brown waters of the stream were fringed with ice, and the ground was iron hard.

The hedgehogs slept deeply, safe in their nest of hay and leaves, and the woman from the house threw more newspapers and sacks over their flowerpot to protect them from the bitter cold. The wind, with ice in its teeth, still blew steadily from the east, and the land cowered under the iron grip of winter. The earth was frozen to a depth of nearly a foot, and the ice had crept along the beaches, freezing the edge of the sea. The birds were unable to find food, and they fell from the air, dead of cold or starvation. Many animals of the wild froze to death in their dens, and the old men shook their heads, saying that such bitter weather had never lasted so long in living memory.

Then spring came. The wind veered west and warm air from the Gulf Stream melted the snow and ice. Every gully and every drain ran merrily with water, and the earth steamed in the sunlight. It was late March, and along the banks of the stream that flowed through The Waste, daffodils and primroses seemed to flower overnight.

The hedgehogs woke up, thin and hungry after the exceptionally long winter, and fed on the slugs and snails that crawled from their winter hiding places. A pair of blackbirds began to build their nest in the hedge above the flowerpot. There was no doubt that the bitter winter was over.

Mattie was now quite tame, and she allowed the woman from the house to pick her up and stroke her when she came for her food. One evening, the woman foolishly carried her into the house and put her on the rug in front of the kitchen fire. Bewildered and frightened, the hedgehog at once curled up into a ball; but after a while, seeing that no immediate danger threatened, she gradually began to uncurl. She was still by no means satisfied that she was safe, and after a quick look around she darted like lightning into the coal scuttle, and there she stayed, quivering with fear.

The woman realized that Mattie did not like being in the house, so she carefully picked her up and took her outside again. The hedgehog then settled down happily to eat her supper, none the worse for her ordeal. The woman never took her into the house again, but sometimes, when the kitchen door was left open, Mattie would quietly creep in of her own accord and lap up a saucer of milk the woman had put down for her.

Both Mattie and Quill had forgotten the previous summer, but as they ranged over the gardens familiar scents reminded them where to find food. They had also forgotten their mother and the old boar, and they ran together, content with each other's company and happy to be alive in a new, adult world.

Under the trees in The Waste, clumps of wild anemones blew in the wind. The damp earth around their roots was full of small creatures, and the two hedgehogs often hunted there, since they had already eaten most of the pests that had remained alive in the gardens after the hard winter.

On a balmy April evening, Mattie, wriggling through a tangle of leaves and grass, came face to face with a strange boar that was hunting alone. The strange hedgehog touched Mattie's snout with his and would have run off with her, but Quill rushed furiously at him, bowling the stranger over again and again and trying to sink his teeth in his throat. The other boar was no match for Quill, who had come through the hard winter in far better condition than his opponent, who had not had the benefit of warm winter quarters and regular meals of bread and milk. The strange hedgehog was soon routed, leaving nothing but a few tufts of his woolly undercoat on the ground.

From then on, Quill always went in front of Mattie. She followed meekly wherever he led, and it was he who chose their hunting grounds and decided when they should go for their bread and milk.

Mattie's first litter was born in May and consisted of four in all: two males and two females. About a week before they were born, a stray cat, sniffing around the flowerpot, had frightened Mattie. The next day, the woman from the house looked into the pot to see if the urchins were safe and was surprised to find that they had gone. Both Mattie and Quill still came regularly for their evening meal of bread and milk, but it seemed to the woman that they had left her garden and gone to live somewhere else. There did not appear to be anywhere in the garden where they could have hidden, and she could not find where they slept during the day, although she looked in all the likely places. Then, for a few evenings, Quill came alone for the bread and milk, and the woman began to fear that Mattie was dead.

Then came an evening when the man from the house, looking through the window of his study, saw Mattie crawling out of a hole behind the compost heap. It was still quite light, and he watched her running up and down the garden for quite a while until eventually she vanished into a tangled mass of convolvulus behind the raspberry canes.

After that, Quill still came alone for his bread and milk, but Mattie was seen at about seven o'clock each evening, scrambling out of her hiding place in the compost heap before taking her exercise in the garden. She was very nervous and curled up when the woman tried to touch her, but late at night her soft grunting could be heard near the house.

Toward the end of June, the woman from the bread and milk house went to see one of her neighbors and found a young hedgehog there, lying unconscious in the sump of a drain. The sides of this sump had been built up to a height of over a foot, so that the water from the downspout would not splash out onto the path, and the little urchin had obviously fallen into it during the night and been unable to climb out.

During the day, two bathfuls of hot water had gushed down onto him. Battered against the sides of the sump and half drowned by the water, he had lain unconscious on the grid for the whole of the afternoon. Blowflies had already settled on his unprotected eyes and on his ears.

When the woman picked him up, water drained from his nose and mouth, but a faint twitching of his limp body told her that he still lived. His bristles were gray, darkening to brown; his snout and paws were black; and his stomach was covered with gray wool. The woman knew that he was about six weeks old.

She carried the little hedgehog by the back legs to let the water drain from his lungs as she took him to the house. When she took him into the house, she dried him as best she could with an old piece of rag, and he rewarded her by pricking her hand as he curled up in terror. After the woman had dried him, she put him deep in the hay of the flowerpot and left some milk outside for him.

The next morning, he was still in the flowerpot, lying half curled up in the hay, with his front paws pressed against his body and his hind feet and tail turned up over them. He was breathing strongly and evenly, but he was still rather damp and his body felt cold. His eyes were tightly closed under his wrinkled brows, and he had not touched the milk.

The woman was determined not to let the young urchin starve to death, so she bought a doll's feeding bottle with a little plastic nipple to feed him with. The weather was cold and damp, so she took him out of the flowerpot and put him in a box with a hot water bottle and plenty of hay. She placed the box near the kitchen stove, and the little hedgehog soon dried out.

That evening, the woman forced the nipple of the feeding bottle between his clenched teeth and managed to squeeze a small quantity of milk and glucose into his mouth. The urchin lay on his back in her hand and swallowed the milk reluctantly.

The next morning, he seemed much stronger. He bit vigorously on the nipple as the woman fed him and watched her every movement with his beady black eyes. He soon recognized the smell of the woman's hands, and he would crawl toward her when she bent to pick him up. He appeared to be quite strong and healthy, but on the fourth day, when the woman picked him up to feed him, she found that his eyes and ears were a crawling mass of maggots. The little hedgehog curled up as soon as the woman tried to brush them away. After a lot of difficulty, she managed to sponge most of the maggots away, but there were still a few left under his lower eyelids, and these could not be dislodged. He let the woman unfold his wrinkled ears and clean them out, and she was able to pick the loose maggots from his fur, but he would not open his eyes, so the woman was unable to tell if they were damaged by the maggots.

He still took his food eagerly, opening the pink cavern of his mouth and chewing vigorously on the nipple as he swallowed the milk and glucose.

The woman decided to let him out for a walk in the garden, where he started to pick up insects from the moss on the path. He was very unsteady on his feet and kept falling over, but apart from this, he seemed quite lively and healthy. When he was put back into his box, he burrowed deeply into the hay, hiding himself from the light.

The woman thought that the little hedgehog would soon be well, but when she went to his box the next day he was lying limply on his side. His breath was coming in great, panting gasps, and by lunchtime he was dead.

Baby hedgehogs that have strayed from their mothers are very difficult to rear. They die of fright, of pneumonia, of general septicemia, from attacks by maggots that literally eat them alive, or simply from grief at the loss of their mothers. They rarely live even as long as a week in captivity; one can only keep them warm, feed them with milk or milk and glucose, and hope that they will not lose the will to live and sink into the apathy that invariably leads to death. If a lost hedgehog has been touched by human hands, its mother has great difficulty in finding it because its scent is overlaid by that of the person who has handled it; so it should be handled as little as possible and put back at once into the nest from which it has strayed, or it will almost certainly die. If a lost urchin is two months old or more, it can live by its own efforts in a garden, especially if some bread and milk is left out for it; but dozens of baby hedgehogs die every year because they stray from their mothers and cannot be found again.

6

THE WEATHER became fine and warm, and day after day, the land basked in unbroken sunshine. The cock blackbird, gleaming in his summer plumage, called, "Aw reet. REET. Aw reet" from the top of an apple tree. The hen taught her four fledglings to take wobbly flights from bough to bough, coaxing them to and fro across the garden of the bread and milk house until, exhausted, they clung precariously to the clothesline, determined to fly no more.

The stream on The Waste shrank to a trickle, and trout lay clearly visible in its shrunken pools, their tails waving in the current like pieces of brown waterweed. A mink, escaped from a fur farm, made his home in one of the banks, and a polecat slunk down from the moor to hunt in the shallows.

The heat wave continued through July, baking the red soil of the gardens pale pink, and when the man from the house watered his beans and peas in the evening, sparrows, thrushes, and blackbirds came and stood in a circle under the fine spray of the hose.

Mattie's three remaining babies grew up strong and healthy. There were not enough slugs and snails left in the gardens to support five hedgehogs, but the dry weather brought with it a plague of cabbage white butterflies, which laid their eggs on the underside of the broccoli and sprouts, and soon there were thousands of juicy green caterpillars for the urchins to feed on. They also fed on ants' eggs, digging into the nests to claw them out, and they went along the rows of broad beans, licking the sweet-tasting blackflies from the leaves and stalks.

Apart from old Bert Smale, their only enemy in the gardens was Stripey, Amelia Dart's lop-eared tomcat. Stripey was growing old; for nearly eleven years he had walked where he pleased, pouncing on birds and field mice and cruelly killing them for sport as well as for food, but lately his muscles had weakened and he had formed the habit of going to the hedgehogs' dish and stealing their bread and milk.

One evening, he stalked into the garden when

Quill and Mattie were eating there with the young hedgehogs and forced his way to the dish, pushing in between Quill and one of the youngsters. All the urchins had frozen at his approach, but now Quill made his bristles stand up and snapped at the cat's face. Stripey spat viciously and slashed at the boar's snout with his claws as Mattie and the three young ones ran off in terror into the shadows.

In the battle that followed, the cat's eyelid was torn, his nose was bitten, and his forepaws were so badly injured by Quill's bristles that he could hardly crawl away. The uninjured boar triumphantly returned to his interrupted feast as the defeated Stripey slunk off, terrified.

After that, the tomcat never went near the bread and milk dish. When he walked down the path of the house, he always kept well away from it, and if he heard the sounds of the hedgehogs feeding, his pace at once quickened until he thought he was out of danger.

When August came, the sultry heat changed to thunder, and storms swept over the country-side. On The Waste, horse mushrooms spread their pink-gilled parasols, which blackened and rotted in the grass. The hedgehogs rooted in the decaying fungi for worms and maggots.

One night, they came across an eel of about

three pounds in weight, which was slithering through the grass, making its way from the lake to the stream. They all pounced on the fish, but neither their teeth nor their claws could get a grip on its slimy skin, and it slid off, unharmed, on its journey to the spawning grounds in the Sargasso sea. The hedgehogs sniffed at the slime the eel had left on the bent grass, and the young ones licked at it. It had a pleasant fishy taste that sharpened their appetites.

They went on to root in the place where the anemones had grown in the spring, and in its rich leaf mold they found some spiders and some small red worms. A gray squirrel, dozing in the fork of a tree, pelted them with twigs, chattering angrily. He thought the hedgehogs were trying to steal his winter store of nuts.

The man from the bread and milk house was fishing in the lake and heard the commotion. He looked up and the night was light enough for him to see the hedgehogs running away, with Quill and Mattie leading the three youngsters as they vanished into the shadows.

Then a big eel took the man's worm and he forgot about the hedgehogs. His light fiberglass rod bent to the pull of the fish and his reel screamed as the line was torn off. The eel made for some sunken tree roots, intending to wrap

its tail around one of them, but the angler managed to turn it before it was able to do so. He played the frantically struggling fish for nearly twenty minutes, and when it slid, exhausted, into his landing net, he was pleased to see that it weighed about four pounds. He severed its vertebrae just behind the head and threw it into a sack, thinking that it would make good eating after it had been stewed in cider and allowed to cool into a jelly.

In early autumn, the hedgehogs started to make their winter home. They carried leaves and hay into the hole behind the compost heap until it was thickly padded; then they made a roof of twigs and leaves and pulled down ivy to form a base. The heaped-up compost sheltered the entrance of their nest from the east winds.

The weather was still fine and warm, and Mattie and her family continued to hunt over the gardens and The Waste while they fattened up for winter. They found that the overripe blackberries which fell from the bushes on The Waste were sweet and juicy, and there were often plump, fruit-fed maggots in the hearts of the berries.

They were feeding on blackberries one night when Playboy lashed out with one of his mighty hoofs and hit one of the young urchins, which flew nearly twenty feet through the air. When the little hedgehog fell to the ground, his back was broken.

The windfalls that fell from the apple trees in the bread and milk garden attracted small black slugs that dug deep into their sides. The hedgehogs found these slugs very tasty, and they nosed among the fallen fruit night after night. The man and his wife often found apples that had been partly gnawed by them in their search for slugs to eat.

The youngsters liked to play with the apples; they loved their smell and the feel of their smooth, shiny skins under their paws. They found that they could roll the windfalls with their snouts, and when the little animals rolled over in play, some of the smaller apples stuck to their spines. They carried two of these interesting toys to their nest and stowed them safely away, just as Mattie and Quill had taken their toys into the flowerpot the year before. The young urchins also took into their nest the broken stub of a pencil and a small bone they had retrieved from the compost heap.

When hedgehogs hibernate, they nearly always hide unlikely objects in their nests. They seem to prefer smooth, round things such as apples and onions, but there is a story of a lonely

urchin that took a worn-out scrubbing brush into its winter quarters and slept curled up against its bristles. In autumn, hedgehogs are very acquisitive and will carry off any movable object they fancy. They are surprisingly strong and can drag off things that are almost as heavy as they are.

Early in October, the rain began. It poured down from the leaden skies until the sodden land could hold no more. Every ditch became a stream, every stream became a river, and every river became a torrent. The four urchins curled up together in their nest, protected from the worst of the weather by their roof of leaves. One evening Mattie was found crouching alone under the weatherboard of the door, waiting for her supper, but she did not come again that year.

7

THE WINTER was short and mild, but very wet. Mattie and her family had not stirred from their nest, and the woman from the house began to wonder if they had come to some harm from the exceptionally wet weather. She wished they had stayed in the flowerpot, where she knew they would have been safe and dry.

In early February, when the sun at last broke through the clouds, she tried to look into the nest, but all she could see was a heap of hay and dried leaves. No warmth was coming from the nest, and she thought that the hedgehogs were probably dead, if, indeed, they were there at all. She did not know that the temperature of hibernating animals is very low and that their heartbeats and respiration slow down, so that they are in a state of suspended animation, which is very like death. If they are awakened suddenly from their winter sleep, they often die of shock. But hedgehogs are only partial hibernators; they sometimes wake of their own accord during a spell of fine weather and hunt for food. Luckily, the woman did not disturb Mattie and her family, and in the last week of March they emerged from the compost heap, none the worse for their winter's sleep.

Mattie made her presence known by snuffling outside the back door of the house one evening. The woman went out and found her sniffing the ground in the place where the bread and milk was usually put. She accepted her supper and allowed the woman to stroke her nose and forehead. Later the same evening, the rest of the family came to feed.

After they had eaten their bread and milk, they played on the concrete terrace for a while, butting each other and scratching the concrete in order to sharpen their claws. Then they ran off into the gathering darkness.

Mattie soon found that she was going to have a second litter, and she drove the two young hedgehogs from the nest. They hung around the gardens for a few days, reluctant to leave their mother. Then they set off to The Waste, where they mated and had families of their own.

Food was plentiful on The Waste, and they

soon forgot about the bread and milk house. All through the summer, they and their young hunted in the grass and bushes around the lake. The men fishing on the lake often saw them and sometimes threw them a small fish to squabble over. The hedgehogs came to know some of the anglers, and although they ran away when a fish or a piece of bread was tossed toward them, they soon crept back to eat it.

When autumn came, they made their winter quarters in a disused rabbit hole on one of the overgrown clay dumps. There was so much rain that winter that the brown flood swirling down from the moor spilled over the banks of the stream, and the lake and the stream became one large expanse of water. The hedgehogs were washed out of their hole by the torrent, and although they swam around for some time, trying to grasp anything that floated within their reach, they gave up one by one, exhausted by their struggles, and their limp bodies were swept down to the sea. Many of the other animals that lived on The Waste lost their lives that winter; the floods were such that pike found their way from the lake into the stream, where they lived and grew fat on the plump, brown trout.

Mattie had her second litter in May, and soon

she was leading them to the dish each evening for a meal of bread and milk. There were three young in the litter, and she ruled them with a rod of iron. When the woman opened the back door of the house, Mattie made the youngsters stand behind her in a line so that only she could be seen in the light which streamed through the open doorway. She also taught them to stand in line with an old garden broom that stood against the wall, so that they looked like a continuation of its bristles.

Quill rarely came to feed at the dish, but he could usually be heard champing snails in the garden, and his path was marked by a wake of broken shells.

One of the young urchins had a tiny pink spot on the tip of her snout where the pigment had not spread evenly. She was a lively little creature, and as she grew older she would let the woman pick her up and fondle her. The people at the house decided to christen her Pinkie.

One evening, the hedgehogs found a rare treat in their dish. Some stewing steak had proved too tough and gristly to cut up, and the woman had put it out for them to eat. They pounced on it, chewing and tearing at it noisily. Pinkie and one of the other youngsters both grabbed the same lump of steak, and a vigorous tug-of-war began; but Pinkie was by far the stronger and the other little hedgehog was soon forced to let go, so suddenly that Pinkie and the meat went head over heels backward. Pinkie did not mind; her bristles protected her as she rolled over, and she had the meat, too.

A young she-cat sometimes came into the garden of the house when Mattie and her family were feeding and eyed them with great interest; she had never seen a hedgehog before. She once crept up to the dish when Mattie was eating and tried to steal some of the milk, but the hedgehog put her bristles up and, when the cat bent to sniff at her, her nose came into contact with their sharp points. The cat gave one howl of pain and fled. She was never seen in the garden again.

Early in July, it was clear that Mattie was going to have yet another litter; the gestation period of hedgehogs is only about six weeks, and a healthy female often has two litters in a year.

Mattie walked slowly and heavily, and she was impatient of the frolics of her three youngsters. She went for her supper of bread and milk earlier than the others did; she could be seen waiting for it at about nine o'clock every evening. If the weather was wet, she sheltered under the weatherboard of the back door, and anyone going out had to open the door very carefully for fear of hurting her.

The three youngsters were now two months old and were able to fend for themselves, but they could not understand why their mother snarled at them and chased them away when they tried to play with her. She snapped at them when they came to feed at the dish, so they gradually left her alone and went to hunt across the gardens by themselves. In the end, Mattie would not let them sleep with her in the hole behind the compost heap, so they wandered out into the lane and found homes for themselves in the hedge.

Pinkie slept in several different places, each further away from the bread and milk house, until she eventually came to the grounds of the Old Hall, where she met a young boar. They ran together for the remainder of the summer and hibernated in a corner of the toolshed from which Tom Endacott had cut the overgrown creepers on the afternoon when he disturbed Mattie's mother. In spring, they mated and founded a new colony of hedgehogs on the grounds of the Old Hall. Sometimes Pinkie and her mate hunted along the lane toward The Waste, and once or twice the woman from the house found Pinkie feeding at the dish, but Mattie and Pinkie met as strangers.

Toward the end of July, Mattie and Quill wandered along the front path of the house and came to the road, which they started to cross, with Quill leading and his mate following some distance behind. When the boar was about halfway across, he felt the ground trembling and heard a great roaring in the distance. He "froze" immediately, but the noise came nearer and nearer. Then there was a blinding light and the earth shook. The noise came nearer still, and Quill panicked. He rushed madly toward the safety of the garden, but he was too late: one of the front wheels of the truck went over him and squashed him flat. When the great noise had roared away into the distance, Mattie left the gutter where she had been cowering and ran out into the road in search of her mate, but she could only recognize him by his smell. She ran back into the garden and crouched, shivering with terror, in the hole behind the compost heap.

Next day, her third litter was born. There were only two babies, and both of them were very puny. Mattie was still terrified by her adventure of the night before, but she washed and suckled her young and kept them warm with her body.

That same evening, Bert Smale's dog found Mattie's nest. He was nosing around in the garden and heard strange sounds coming from the compost heap, so he stuck his nose as far into the hole as it would go and scrabbled at the leaves with his paws. The hole was too small for him to force his way into the nest, but Mattie could see his face and feel his hot breath on her. The dog barked again and again, daring her to come out, and his tongue drooled saliva onto the sill of the nest.

The commotion brought the man to the back door of the house, and he chased Bert's dog away. Mattie stood tense, with her bristles up, guarding the entrance to her nest; although she was trembling with fright, she would not curl up and leave her babies unprotected. She stood motionless for a long time, looking warily out of the nest and making little spitting sounds. Then she turned and ate her young, as hedgehogs will if they are frightened or worried during or immediately after the time when a litter is born.

8

MATTIE no longer slept in the hole behind the compost heap. A spider wove its web across the entrance of the nest, and the woman from the house noticed that the threads remained unbroken. Each morning, the hedgehogs' bread and milk was found untouched, and the silvery trails of snails began to shine on the garden paths.

Mattie was living deep in the heart of a patch of nettles on The Waste; although the fright she had had after the birth of her latest litter had become a dim memory, she still avoided the gardens.

During the month of August, she hunted alone on the banks of the lake. Summer had burned itself out with the end of July, and the nights were cool and cloudy. The chill in the air reminded the hedgehog that winter was on its way, and she started to make a nest in a blackberry thicket; but one night she smelled the hated scent of badger near the entrance of the tunnel she had made through the long grass. She had never seen a badger, but she knew that its scent meant danger, so she set off under the star-laden sky to the safety of her old, familiar hunting grounds.

Next morning, Amelia Dart told her neighbors that she had been awakened by a strange scratching sound during the night. She had looked out of her window, she said, and there in the moonlight she had seen "a fuzzy-peg a-sliding up and down my old chickun-'ouse door."

Amelia had a dismantled hen coop leaning against the hedge in her back garden. Its rotting wood was covered with green and yellow lichen, and at night wood lice ran over it in their hundreds and slugs crawled around its base. Mattie had spent the night climbing up the door of this old chicken house, feeding on wood lice as she went, then curling herself up into a ball and sliding down again. After gorging herself on the wood lice, she had slept all day in the double hedge near the spot where she was born.

The familiar scents awoke old memories, and the next evening Mattie ran to the bread and milk house and grunted outside the back door for her supper.

The flowerpot was still full of leaves and hay and the inside was warm and dry, so she started to prepare it for hibernation. The man from the house brought some more hay and left it in the garden near the pot, and each night Mattie carried mouthfuls of it into her winter quarters until the flowerpot was so full that there was hardly room for her to squeeze in.

In mid-September, she settled down for her winter sleep. It was the first time she had hibernated alone, but the flowerpot was so cozy that she did not miss the other hedgehogs.

She only came out once during the winter, and the woman saw her rooting in the dead leaves under the sycamore tree and gave her some bread and milk.

That winter was mild but very wet, and Mattie woke early in the spring. Although it was only the first week of March, the weather was warm and sunny. The blackbirds were building their mud-lined nest in the hedge above the flowerpot, and Mattie woke to their song. She felt dazed and hungry after her long sleep, and she had forgotten all the unpleasant things that had happened to her during the previous summer. Slugs and snails had survived the mild winter in their thousands, so there was plenty of food in the gardens for her, but she always had her meal of bread and milk before she set out for her night's hunting. Like all hedgehogs, she had an enormous appetite.

One night toward the end of March, she came across a strange hedgehog hunting in the double hedge along the lane, a young boar who had been driven away from home by his mother. After crossing several fields and crawling through a number of hedges, he had picked up Mattie's scent. For three nights he had hung around the lane; he was afraid of the scent of humans and would not go into the gardens in search of her.

Mattie was now three years old and past the prime of her life; few wild hedgehogs live longer than three years because the hazards of their existence are so great. Sometimes an exceptionally strong and healthy specimen like Mattie's father, the old boar, will live to the age of five or six, but this is very unusual. Mattie was beginning to feel old.

She greeted the young boar without much enthusiasm, touching his snout with hers and following where he led. They ran together for several weeks, but the boar was wild and Mattie was half tame; she liked to hunt in the safety of the gardens and he wanted the wildness of The Waste. They slept in a nest they made in the double hedge, and there Mattie's young were born in the first week of May. There were five of them: three females and two males, the largest litter she had had. As soon as the youngsters were old enough, Mattie took them for a feed of bread and milk each evening.

Her mate hunted alone and would not go with his family to the bread and milk dish. They saw him less and less often until in the end he went to live on The Waste, where he soon mated with another sow and was never again seen in the gardens.

Mattie was now on very friendly terms with the woman of the house. She no longer put up her bristles when she came to feed at the dish; she slicked them down so that in the half-light her back looked as if it were covered with coarse hair. She was very proud of her five babies and she allowed the woman to handle them freely. The little hedgehogs were fat and healthy. They gorged themselves on bread and milk every evening; then they played on the concrete terrace of the house, belching contentedly, until Mattie led them away to hunt over the gardens.

One evening, they found a sparrow's nest that had been torn out of the hedge by Amelia Dart's cat. Four blue eggs were smashed on the ground, and the hedgehogs lapped up the broken yolks and found them good to eat. None of them had tasted eggs until then.

A few days later, Mattie crawled under the wire netting of Jack Belton's hen run soon after dawn and found a newly laid egg in the nest box. Its smell reminded her of the tasty feed she and her young ones had had from the sparrow's eggs, but try as she would she could not open her mouth wide enough to crack the shell and she could not roll the egg out of the box to break it. She gave up in disgust.

Hedgehogs will eat hens' eggs that are laid "wild" if they can roll them down a slope and break them. They also steal birds' eggs at times, but only if the nest is built low enough for them to reach; they are good climbers, but they seldom go to the trouble of robbing a nest that is not easily accessible. They can usually find all the food they want on the ground.

It is sometimes said that hedgehogs eat pheasants' eggs, but this is not true. A hen pheasant is well able to protect her family, and she will peck out the eyes of any animal rash enough to try to steal her eggs or her young.

Mattie's family grew up without any mishaps. By the end of June, they were able to hunt on

their own, and their mother usually went alone to the bread and milk dish. She slept in the flowerpot again, and the youngsters lay wherever they chose—sometimes they slept in the double hedge and sometimes in a patch of pampas grass in Amelia Dart's garden.

It was a beautiful summer: the days were still and sunny and the nights were lit by a million stars. There was a bumper strawberry crop, and the woman from the bread and milk house covered hers with pieces of old net curtain material to protect them from the birds. At night, the sun-soaked fruit gave off a warm, sweet smell that attracted the young hedgehogs, and they came and poked their heads under the nets to steal a few berries.

One morning, the woman found one of the young urchins with a piece of curtain net wound round and round his body. His bristles had caught in the material, and in his efforts to break free, the little thief had nearly strangled himself. She soon cut the net away, and the little hedgehog scampered off, none the worse for his adventure.

At the end of the lane, where The Waste began, there was an old, tumbledown stone wall that had originally marked the boundary of the clay company's land. Years of wind, rain, and frost had fretted away the mortar, and the stones were perched precariously on each other. Each winter, when the frosts came, they caused a bit of the wall to collapse, and the spaces left between the stones provided hiding places for snails. In dry weather the hedgehogs could usually find food there.

Mattie and her family were scrambling about on this wall one night in July. The stones were still warm from the sun, and the hedgehogs were happily crawling in and out of the gaps in the wall, picking up snails as they went. Mattie found a larger cluster of snails glued together in a hollow near the top of the wall, but she was unable to reach them with her snout or her paws, so she started to scratch at the mortar with her claws. It was old and rotten, and she soon scraped away so much that she was almost able to reach the snails. Then there was a sharp cracking sound, and she fell heavily to the ground, a big stone coming down at the same time. The hedgehog had no time to curl up to protect herself from injury, and the stone hit one of her hind legs and broke it like a stick.

Mattie lay on the ground, half stunned. She tried to curl up but a terrible pain shot through her leg when she tried to fold it against her body. She could not understand what had happened to her, and she was too frightened to move. The youngsters had run off in terror when the stone fell, and she lay there alone until dawn, when the sky, brightening in the east, warned her that she must hide.

Limping painfully on three legs, she dragged herself slowly along the lane. Her broken leg dangled helplessly, and when it touched the ground, spasms of pain shot through her body. Her eyes dazzled by the morning light, she limped awkwardly along, and it was nearly noon when at last she crawled under the garden gate and reached the safety of the flowerpot.

∾9∾

THE WOMAN from the house was hanging out her washing when she saw Mattie dragging herhelf across the onion patch toward the flowerpot, and she realized that the hedgehog had been injured. She thought at first that Mattie had been run over by a car.

The injured hedgehog crawled painfully into the flowerpot, and the woman brought her husband, who put his hand into the hay to lift Mattie out; but she was frantic with pain and fear and snapped at the man's hand. Then she tried to curl up, but she was in such pain that she was unable to do so.

The man carefully lifted her out, managing to avoid being bitten by the terrified hedgehog, and the woman tried to straighten the injured leg as gently as she could, while Mattie lay on her side panting, limp with exhaustion. The upper bone of the leg had snapped, and the end of it had pierced the skin. Already flies were settling on the wound.

The hedgehog seemed at last to be unconscious, so the woman pulled the broken bone straight and sponged the wound with a mild disinfectant. She then set the leg in small, padded splints, which she bound firmly in place with strips of bandage. By then, Mattie was breathing more easily and seemed more comfortable. After a while, she regained consciousness, and the woman gave her a saucer of bread and milk, liberally laced with brandy. After a moment's hesitation, the hedgehog discovered that she was ravenously hungry, and holding her injured leg stiffly behind her, she ate her fill. The fumes of the brandy rose to her head, and soon she was sleeping deeply, so the man picked her up and put her into the flowerpot, seeing that she was covered with hay in case her injury caused her to feel cold.

Mattie slept all that day and all that night; then, early the next morning, she crawled to the back door of the house to see if any bread and milk had been put out for her. The woman fed her and tenderly carried her back to the flowerpot.

It was obvious that the hedgehog would not

be able to find her own food for several weeks, so the man decided to make her a hutch so that she could live beside the house where he and his wife could look after her. The hutch had a hinged roof and a screen door with a narrow entrance to protect its inmate from cats. The walls and the roof were made snug and waterproof with roofing felt, and the woman filled Mattie's new home with hay. They put the hedgehog in, and she burrowed into the hay and went to sleep.

Mattie soon got used to the hutch and accepted it as her home. Every morning and every evening, the woman brought a dish of food to the door and called Mattie's name. The hedgehog quickly learned that the call meant food and came out as soon as she heard it. The splints remained securely fastened to her leg, so the woman did not touch them.

As the days went by, it became clear that Mattie was no longer in pain, although she was still unable to use the injured leg. She spent most of her time sleeping and eating, and the woman found that she liked a wide variety of foods, but junket, baked custard, eggs, and sour milk were her favorites. Mattie also liked meat, either raw or cooked, cheese, bacon rind, currants, and sultanas. She often ate the scraps left over from meals, and she was very fond of fatty things such as suet pudding. She did not try to hunt at night, but she often crawled about on the concrete terrace of the house during the day, picking up ants and other small insects.

Early in September, the woman cut the splints away from the hedgehog's injured leg. The wound had healed completely, but there was a lump where the bone had not set straight. Mattie carefully put her foot to the ground and limped back into her hutch. The mended leg seemed stiff and unmanageable at first, but as time went on the hedgehog found that she could use it again, although she walked stiffly for the remainder of her life.

The time for hibernation arrived, but Mattie seemed quite content to stay in her hutch, and as the weather grew colder she collected leaves that had fallen from the sycamore tree and carried them, mouthful by mouthful, into the hutch. When the nights grew cold and frosty, she burrowed deep into the leaves and hay and curled herself up to sleep the winter away.

Meanwhile, her latest litter had scattered. Some were living in the gardens, and some were living in the double hedge along the lane, where they hibernated in nests lined with grass and leaves.

The pampas grass in Amelia Dart's garden was growing very untidy, so she decided to set fire to it. As the flames spread through the tinder-dry grass, two sleepy young hedgehogs rushed out with their bristles on fire. They died of shock; there was nothing Amella could do for them. The rest of Mattie's latest litter lived through the winter to wander across the fields when spring came. They mated and raised families and lived and died as hedgehogs always have.

Mattie awoke early in April. At the beginning of her hibernation she had measured ten inches from head to tail and had weighed one pound thirteen ounces. Her length had not changed, but she had lost ten ounces in weight; she had lived on her fat during her winter sleep. She ate enormously, and soon rolls of fat could be felt under the brown wool of her stomach. She allowed the woman from the house to turn her on her back and tickle her stomach, and she liked having her snout and forehead stroked; but she made it quite clear that these liberties could only be taken with her permission. She was content to live in her hutch, but she seemed determined to retain all her rights as a wild animal. She did not always answer to her name, and she sometimes slept away from her hutch for a night or two; but she never missed going to the back door of the house for her bread and milk. She did not mate that year, although she hunted over the gardens in company with several other hedgehogs.

When summer came, the woman often sat in a deck chair on the concrete terrace of the house. Sometimes she brought her knitting out with her, and Mattie would often creep from her hutch to crouch in the shade of the deck chair. She liked to play with one of the balls of wool, and would trundle it to and fro until the strands were tangled round and round her bristles. Then she would stand still, waiting impatiently to be freed.

Mattie liked the sunshine, but it seemed to hurt her eyes; her sight, like that of all hedgehogs, was poor by day but keen at night. When she sat in the sun, she would wrinkle her brows over her eyes, trusting to her sense of smell to warn her of any danger that approached. Her face bore an expression of meek resignation.

When her food was put out, Mattie would put up her bristles and threaten any strange hedgehog that came near her dish, and she would not allow any other animal to approach her hutch.

She gave the people of the house such affection as was in her nature, but it was clear that she regarded them mainly as sources of food and comfort; she knew that the call of "Mattie" meant that some tidbit was being held out for her to take. When the woman stroked her snout and stomach, she felt again the warmth of her mother's tongue licking her and she was soothed and comforted. The scent trails in the gardens brought back memories of other summers, and the smell of the cows in the meadow spoke to her of milk. She did not remember the many young hedgehogs she had brought into the world, and the pains she had suffered were either forgotten or remembered only as slight discomforts.

The long hot summer passed slowly while Mattie dozed the days away and wandered over the gardens in the early evening. She liked to walk along the double rows of broad beans, picking insects from the plants. She ate the slugs in the strawberry patch and the greenfly in the mint bed; she kept the garden free of every kind of pest.

The blackbirds knew her, and they sat on the clothesline, watching her as she rooted in the grass under the apple trees or picked caterpillars from the broccoli. They saw her matronly figure stumping across the lawn to scratch the eggs from an ant's nest or to steal an occasional strawberry from under the nets. Sometimes they swooped down on Mattie's dish and stole her bread and milk. If she caught them doing this, she would advance on them indignantly, grunting loudly.

She aged noticeably during the summer, and when September came she was glad to settle down early for her winter sleep. She carried a few treasures into the hutch, wrapped herself in hay, and slept deeply until the following spring.

⌐⌐**10**⌐⌐

MATTIE was in her sixth year. Her bristles were grizzled and lifeless, the wool on her lower jaw had turned white, and the long golden hair on her flanks had faded to a dirty yellow. Her sense of smell was still fairly keen, but her hearing was failing and she was nearly blind. That spring, she did not hunt in the gardens; she regarded her bread and milk as her only food, and slugs and snails often crawled across the concrete terrace of the house within a few feet of her, but she took no notice of them. When the woman called her by name, she would waddle out of the hutch and shake her head confusedly as she tried to locate the sound. Sometimes she would even turn and wander off in the wrong direction.

She liked to lie in the sun outside her hutch; she seemed to be constantly tired. At night she slept deeply. She was respected and feared by all the cats of the neighborhood; most of them had learned long ago that they were not welcome in Mattie's garden, and she soon frightened off the few that did dare to venture in.

Sometimes, Pinkie would come into the garden at dusk, looking for food with her children and grandchildren. Mattie would watch them as they ran in and out of the shadows, jostling and playing like children just let out of school, but if any of them came near her dish she would put up her bristles and snarl at them until they went away.

All through the summer, Mattie ate and slept. Sometimes, in the strawberry season, she walked down to the strawberry bed and lay basking in the sunshine among the sweet-smelling fruit. On moonlit nights she would sometimes wander, her bristles tipped with silver, along the rows of broad beans, but she soon returned to her hutch and went to sleep.

The hot August days made her restless, and she sometimes wandered up the garden to the apple trees, where she nosed among the hard, green apples that had fallen to the ground, but she could never manage to get at the slugs in them.

Like all wild animals, a hedgehog, when it

knows it is going to die, will crawl away to a quiet place. So it was with Mattie.

One afternoon in early autumn, the woman from the house stood watching a fungus grow on the damp wood of the gate leading into the lane. First, there was a dark stain on the wood, then a bubble that hardened into a little fungus which grew and spread.

The woman wondered at the miracle of life. She thought of Mattie and how she, who had once been wild, was now so tame. She saw Mattie coming along the garden path and called her name, but the hedgehog took no notice and continued on her way along the lane.

Swallows were gathering on the telegraph wires, and crows were fluttering above the new stubble like pieces of charred paper in the wind. Every golden leaf drifting to the ground spoke of autumn, but Mattie was not preparing to hibernate.

She stood for a while in the lane, her old nose scenting the west wind, which blew from The Waste and brought with it the scent of heather, of pond water, and of cows and grass. The scents reminded Mattie of frogs and fish, of blackberries, and of warm milk oozing from the udders of the cows in the meadow. She remembered Quill and how they had hunted together across the gardens, along the lane, and over The Waste. Her nostrils twitched, and she went on along the lane.

Slowly, staggering a little, she limped on. Once or twice, she overbalanced into the gutter, but she managed to scramble out again and crawled on, panting, until she reached the rough grass by the old stone wall at the end of the lane.

She skirted the meadow where the cows lay. Playboy was at the far end of the meadow, but he did not see her as she crawled under the fence and into The Waste.

The grass was very long and thick, and Mattie found it very hard to crawl through. She came to the lake and rested for a while at the place where, long ago, the old boar and his mate had fought the adder. A kingfisher flashed like blue fire over the water, and a pike lay close to a clump of reeds.

She crossed the patch of clay where Quill had fallen into the lake, but the ground was dry and hard, and she did not slip.

An angler saw her making her purposeful way around the lake. He watched her lift her snout as she caught the scent of leaf mold, and then she crawled into a patch of nettles, where she rested for a while. The earth was dark and cool, and memories came flooding back to her

with its remembered odor. She turned her head this way and that, savoring long-forgotten scents.

Mattie left the patch of nettles and came to some blackberry bushes. The purple fruit lay squashed on the ground, but the hedgehog took no notice of it; she pushed her way slowly through the grass and brambles to the center of the thickest bush.

Jays screeched in the hazels and an otter padded along the edge of the stream. Mattie was very tired; her chest was almost bursting as she gasped for breath.

She came at last to a pile of drifted leaves deep in the heart of the brambles. The leaves were warm and dry; they reminded her of the nest in the tree stump where she was born, and she burrowed gratefully into them, seeking the comfort of their warmth. Lying half curled up on her side in the dappled shade, she heard the sparrows twittering overhead. The sound of their song blended with a gentle buzzing in her ears as the world swam dizzily into eternal night.